DREAMS

MADE EASY

DREAMS

MADE EASY

Sarah Dening

GODSFIELD PRESS

Published in 1999 by Sterling Publishing
Company, Inc. 387 Park Avenue South,
New York, N.Y. 10016

Distributed in Canada by Sterling
Publishingc/o Canadian Manda Group,
One Atlantic Avenue, Suite 105
Toronto, Ontario, Canada M6K 3E7
Distributed in Australia by Capricorn
Link (Australia) Pty Ltd
P O. Box 6651, Baulkham Hills, Business
Centre, NSW 2153, Australia

Printed and bound in Hong Kong
Sterling ISBN 0-8069-9853-9

Dedication:
I SHOULD LIKE TO THANK PATRICK DYER
FOR MANY INVALUABLE SUGGESTIONS THAT
HELPED ME BRING ORDER OUT OF CHAOS.

Library of Congress Cataloging-in-Publication Data
Denning, Sarah.
  Dreams made easy : an introduction to the basics of
the ancient art of dream interpretation / Sarah Dening.
    p.   cm.
  Includes index.
  ISBN 0-8069-9853-9
  1. Dream interpretation.   I. Title.
BF1091.D45   1999
154.6'3--dc21
                                            99-20770
                                                 CIP

10 9 8 7 6 5 4 3 2 1

ACKNOWLEDGEMENTS
*The publishers wish to thank the
following for the use of pictures:*
AKG London: 7, 21, 33t, 42b,
54c, 62tl, 63t 74br
Allsport: 68tl, 69
Bridgeman Art Library: 12tl, 13;
Bruce Coleman Ltd: 34, 56tl, 57tr, 65b;
Mary Evans Picture Library: 46tl, 47
Eye Ubiquitous: 29b
Sally and Richard Greenhill: 38;
Richard Harding Picture
Library: 39b, 53b
Image Bank: 40–1b, 50c, b, 62b, 66b, 70b
Images Colour Library: 6, 14b, 36tl, 37,
39c, 64tl, 65t, 66tl, 67b, 67t
Popperfoto: 20tl, 21b
Tony Stone Images: 22, 40bl, 42tl, 43t,
48tl, 55br, 61t, 63b, 68b

Illustrations:
Rachel Fuller, Lorraine Harrison,
Ivan Hissey, Rhian Nest-James

Photography:
Ian Parsons

Contents

Introduction

Dreams are like treasures hidden within your inner world. They can help with your problems, provide insight into relationships, heal past wounds, and be a signpost to the future without delay.

Above: Are you at a cross-roads in life? Your dreams may have an answer.

To find the treasure, you have to dig beneath the surface and be open to whatever you find. In the process, you can gain greater understanding of what makes you tick. This brings many positive benefits in terms of your outlook and personality. The most troubling dreams can sometimes bring the greatest healing. Recurring dreams draw your

Above: Use your dreams to help you understand what is going on in your relationships.

made

attention to long-stand-ing issues which must be resolved so that you can move on. Night-mares are nature's shock treatment, urging you to recognize a source of acute stress and to take immediate remedial action.

Above: **Nightmares are an unpleasant jolt, but can give insight into worries.**

Whatever their content, your dreams have an ultimately benevolent aim: to act as your own inner guide or wise counselor as you journey through life in search of love and fulfillment. Dreams can be exciting, mysterious, or maddening, but always infinitely rewarding.

How to Remember Dreams

Scientists investigating sleep have proved that we all dream.
When you are dreaming, your eyes move around beneath your
closed eyelids. This is known as Rapid Eye Movement, or REM
sleep, and occurs at regular intervals throughout the night.

**A SKILL YOU
CAN LEARN**
Some people find it easier than others to recall their dreams. Research indicates that if you have an extroverted personality, or a very rational, analytical approach to life, you are less likely to remember your dreams than your more introverted or intuitive friends. Please do not feel discouraged, though. Practice the following "Five Golden Rules" – and you, too, can succeed in recalling the drama which is performed every night in the inner theater of your psyche.

Above: Extroverts do not tend to remember dreams easily and must practice the art.

Left: Quieter personalities often recall their dreams without difficulty and in great detail.

Below: **Give yourself the best chance of remembering a dream accurately when you wake by being well prepared.**

TOOLS FOR RECORDING DREAMS

- a special notebook that will become your dream journal
- a pen or pencil, placed within easy reach of your bed
- a bedside lamp

The Five Golden Rules for Remembering Your Dreams

You can develop your ability to remember your dreams — it just takes a little practice in following a simple routine. Get into the habit of making notes as soon as you wake: you will find that you soon build up a fascinating journal.

1 Relax before you go to bed. Being busy until bedtime inhibits dream recall. as do stimulants like coffee and alcohol.

Left: A quiet read before bed is a good way of winding down, giving the best chance of dream recall.

2 As you drift off to sleep, affirm to yourself: "When I wake up, I shall remember a dream."
3 Once awake, lie still, keep your eyes closed, and drift back until you capture perhaps a fragment of a dream or just a single image. Keep stray thoughts about the day to come firmly out of your mind.

made

4 Reach for your journal, moving as little as possible. Shifting your position can make a dream disappear. Write down what you remember, using the present tense to bring it alive again. If nothing comes to mind, make a note of your thoughts or feelings as you awake.

5 Stay motivated! Dream recall is a creative endeavor that needs daily practice. The more attention you give your dreams, the more rewarding they will be.

Interpreting Your Dreams

Think of your dream as a movie whose story is your life, whose characters are aspects of your personality and whose setting provides the emotional backdrop. It is a coded message about something you are unaware of – but need to know.

THE SYMBOLIC LANGUAGE OF DREAMS

Cracking the code takes a little effort. Each image in the dream, whether person, animal, or object, is a symbol of special relevance to you. Because a symbol can have many different meanings, its significance in your dream depends on the feelings and memories you associate with it. To find out more about any dream symbol, look at the box (right) entitled "Interpreting Symbols," and ask yourself the questions listed.

Above: **Snakes in dreams can represent sexuality – or wisdom.**

INTERPRETING SYMBOLS

• How would I describe the image to somebody who has never seen it before?

• What do I feel about it?

• Does it remind me of anybody?

• Does it remind me of a situation, past or present, that I need to resolve?

• Did something happen recently that may have triggered this image?

IS THERE ALWAYS AN EASY ESCAPE ROUTE IF RESPONSIBILITIES BECOME TOO MUCH?

IS ESCAPE THE ANSWER? DOES TOO MUCH FREEDOM CAUSE PAIN?

IS THIS RELATIONSHIP LIKE A PROTECTIVE BUBBLE OR A SUFFOCATING PRISON?

DOES DECAY THREATEN TO DESTROY THINGS AND UNDERMINE SECURITY?

Above: **Seemingly bizarre features of a dream may have relevance to your life.**

Already, you may have begun to understand what the dream is about. Beware, though, of explanations that are too simple or too literal. Don't jump to conclusions before you have used some further tools for exploring dreams:

WAYS TO EXPLORE DREAMS

- Have a discussion with the "you" who features in the dream. Ask how he or she feels. Now describe the situation from your waking point of view.

- Imagine the dream from the standpoint of each of the other characters. How does it feel to be that person (or animal)? What is their attitude to you? Have they any advice to offer?

- Make simple drawings of images you feel strongly about.

How will you know when you have found the right meaning? When the message strikes home, it is as though an inner voice says, "Aha! That's it!" – and you know in your bones that you're there. Learn to trust your instinct.

Dream People

TThe people in your dreams usually represent aspects of your own nature which you may be unaware of or prefer not to know. Admitting them into your life enhances your relationship with yourself and others.

Male figures symbolize the masculine, assertive, goal-oriented side of yourself, while females signify your feminine, receptive, sensitive qualities.

Left: **The sex of the person you dream about may represent aspects of your own nature.**

FAMILY

Dreams about family members occupy a special category. Brothers and sisters, in particular, can sometimes represent those sides of yourself that you rarely express. Often, though, the purpose of these dreams is to provide insight into family relationships. By shedding new light on difficult issues, your dream can help to heal conflicts.

YOUR PARENTS AND YOUR SELF

Dreams about your father or mother may reflect your actual experience of them. Otherwise, they symbolize the maternal or paternal side of yourself. Is the

A sibling in a dream
may be a metaphor
for a hidden side
of yourself.

mother in your dream supportive
and loving – or controlling and
smothering? Is the father reliable
and protective or judgmental and
authoritarian? What does your
dream tell you about your relationship with these figures?

WISE ELDERS

Grandparents in dreams are often
the embodiment of wisdom or
spiritual insight. If your childhood was unhappy, a dream
grandparent may help you to
experience the love you lacked.

Friends and Strangers

Friends and strangers who feature in your dreams symbolize parts of your own nature from which you are cut off. What inhibits you from expressing the qualities which you admire or envy in a dream figure? Do you need to overcome false modesty or feelings of unworthiness?

ADVANTAGES IN DISGUISE

Accepting that you possess character traits that you dislike in others may be galling. Yet sometimes these are the very qualities you most need.

Above: A friend may represent characteristics you wish you had yourself.

A dream that features a friend whose ruthlessness you secretly admire could mean you would benefit from being tougher. Let your dreams help you become the person you truly are.

made
easy

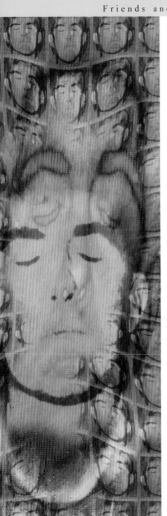

NOT SO VERY STRANGE

Strangers in dreams represent aspects of personality which are so deeply hidden within yourself that you do not identify with them. Such dreams indicate that you are now ready to admit to these traits. Sometimes all you need do is accept them as being part of human nature.

FRIENDS AND STRANGERS

Because the people in your dreams usually embody aspects of yourself, it's important not to judge them. The figure you fear or dislike may prove an invaluable ally in a bad situation.

If you dream of being envious of someone, ask yourself exactly what it is about them that you would like to have, or to be. Experience shows that if you can dream it, you can usually have it – or be it!

Left: **Your most deeply buried traits may surface in the guise of a stranger who appears in your dream.**

Children and Babies

> Dreams about children and babies often indicate new
> beginnings. You may be starting a new relationship or
> project, or developing a different perspective.

How old is the child? If it is five, what happened five years ago that could be relevant now? Are there unresolved issues dating back to when you were five?

CHILDREN

Your "inner child" can symbolize openness, playfulness, or the ability to live in the present. Less positively, it can suggest childishness. If the child is neglected, the dream is urging you to acknowledge and nurture whatever it represents for you. A young boy can denote new creative activity; a little girl may imply newly discovered feelings or new relationships. A child can sometimes represent your innermost self.

Left: The age of a dream child could point to the events in your life at the time she was born.

easy

Above: **Dreams of children can imply a need to be less inhibited and more enthusiastic.**

BABIES

In symbolic language, babies represent new potential, perhaps a project or a relationship still in its infancy. They can also suggest feelings of vulnerability and the need to take special care of yourself.

Left: **Babies epitomize the birth of a relationship or project, or signify fragility.**

Celebrities and Royalty

Dreaming of famous people may simply suggest that your
life lacks glamour or romance. Do you yearn for excitement?
Do you secretly hope that some day your prince (or princess)
will come? Your dream may also indicate a wish for greater
recognition in your work or personal life.

WHOSE GREATNESS?

Dreams featuring celebrities are
often a message about learning
to follow your own star. What
does this person represent to
you? It is easy to project onto
somebody famous qualities that
are essentially your own. It is
harder, but infinitely more
rewarding, to work at realizing
them in your own life.

POWER AND GLORY

Royal personages, originally considered sacred, still command
fascination. In dreams they signify
the authority and dignity which
are the hallmark of a mature individual. A king, often associated
with leadership, represents the

Above: **Is there a daring extrovert
lurking at the back of your psyche,
waiting to wow the world?**

made
easy

quintessence of masculinity. A queen symbolizes the supremely feminine qualities of feeling and relatedness. Princes and princesses may suggest latent "royal" attributes.

CELEBRITIES AND

In a man's dream the queen represents feminine power, or even his mother. In a woman's dream, a meeting with a queen indicates whether she is comfortable with her own authority.

Below: **Do you see yourself as a follower or a star deserving acclaim and reward?**

E GANG'S ALL HERE

Weddings

Dreams of weddings suggest the possibility of a union between
the masculine and feminine sides of yourself, so that head and
heart form an equal partnership. Medieval alchemists called
this state of psychological wholeness the "inner marriage."
Your dream may therefore be symbolic of your commitment
to becoming a complete human being.

Above: **The perfect union. Wedding
dreams indicate harmony between
different sides of your character.**

THE BRIDE ALONE

In one "wedding" dream familiar
to many women, the bridegroom
fails to appear. This may signify
that you feel ready for marriage
but cannot find a suitable
man. More commonly, it
is a message that the masculine aspect of your
nature is underdeveloped.

WHO IS YOUR
INNER PARTNER?

If you dream about mar-
rying your parent, ask
yourself whether you have always
been a "daddy's girl" or a "mama's
boy." A dream in which you marry
a former lover can indicate that
you have now managed to integrate into yourself those qualities
that you found attractive in him or
her. Use the section on "sexuality"
to help you understand more.

BLACK WEDDING?

If the bride wears black in a dream, she represents the "dark," powerful feminine aspect of your personality. This is the part of your nature that can stand up for her deepest feelings and say "no" rather than seek to please. Such a dream suggests that you need to – or perhaps are about to – become more intimately wedded to this aspect of yourself. The result may be a significant change in the way you approach relationships.

Below: **Deserted at the altar? Maybe a nightmare, but more likely to indicate a need to cultivate your masculine side.**

Houses

Think of yourself as a house. There are dark corners, neglected areas, or neat and clean rooms for public gaze. The rooms represent different aspects of yourself. The exterior symbolizes the face you present to the world. Dreaming about your childhood home may indicate that in some respect you are still childlike.

BATHROOMS AND TOILETS

Bathrooms in dreams are places of purification where you "wash away" negative, spiritually impov- erished attitudes. Dreams set in bathrooms therefore imply that you have the capacity to live more closely in accordance with your innate nature. First, though, you must find a way of "cleaning up your act."

LETTING GO

Many people dream about being unable to find a restroom or discovering that the available toilets are blocked up. This suggests

Left: Facets of your personality can be compared to the rooms in a house, with both private and public areas.

A dream set in your childhood home may be highlighting an immature aspect of your psyche.

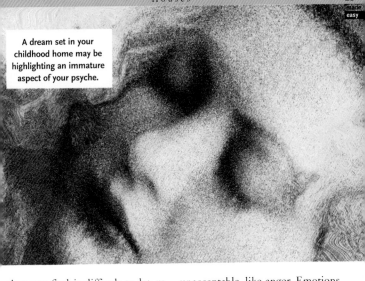

that you find it difficult to let go and express yourself spontaneously. Such dreams may also indicate that you are repressing your creative side.

NO PRIVACY

A toilet with no door implies a fear of exposing private thoughts or feelings that you consider to be unacceptable, like anger. Emotions that you keep bottled up will try to find an outlet in your dreams. This dream can be a message that you are too concerned about what other people think.

Left: **Exposed to public gaze! Are you anxious about revealing your true feelings?**

Kitchens and Eating

In kitchens, raw ingredients are turned into nourishing meals. Dreams about kitchens therefore indicate that a process of transformation is taking place within your personality. Something in your life is currently "hot" and needs attention. Ask yourself, "What's cooking?"

NEW PERSPECTIVES

Dreams set in your own kitchen imply that your view of yourself is undergoing a change. Those featuring somebody else's kitchen suggest a need to reconsider your attitude toward that person.

Above: The heart of the home: kitchen dreams are linked to altered perceptions.

SOUL FOOD

Eating in dreams implies assimilating the properties represented by the particular food. Meat, traditionally considered appropriate nourishment for heroes, stands for red-blooded, assertive, goal-oriented attitudes. Dairy products symbolize feminine, nurturing qualities, "the milk of human-kindness," while vegetables indicate a natural growth process.

ARE YOU STARVING – OR GREEDY?

Your feelings about the food indicate whether you are getting the emotional and spiritual sustenance you need. Do you feel guilty about eating it? Is it satisfying, sweet, or difficult to chew?

Above: **An obsessive relationship with food can reflect a yearning for emotional security.**

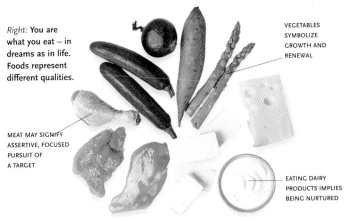

Right: **You are what you eat – in dreams as in life. Foods represent different qualities.**

VEGETABLES SYMBOLIZE GROWTH AND RENEWAL

MEAT MAY SIGNIFY ASSERTIVE, FOCUSED PURSUIT OF A TARGET

EATING DAIRY PRODUCTS IMPLIES BEING NURTURED

Finding New Rooms

To dream about finding a new room is a cause for celebration.
The dream is a message that there is more to you than you
think! Finding a new room implies unlocking hidden potential.
This dream invites you to experience the joy of discovering
new talents and abilities.

THE INTERIOR DECOR

Is your newly discovered
room clean and ready for
immediate occupation, or
dilapidated and in need of
work? An empty room sig-
nifies the unlimited
possibilities of a fresh start.
Old, shabby furniture may
represent outworn atti-
tudes, perhaps inherited
from previous generations.
How do you feel about
this room?

WHAT IS ITS PURPOSE?

Finding a new bedroom suggests a
fresh approach to close relationships or perhaps renewed sexual
vigor. If you are lucky enough to

Above: Discovering a new room
is an exciting moment and heralds
great things. You are being invited
to explore your hidden potential,
in a spirit of adventure.

find an entire new wing in a house you thought you knew well, you can look forward to a period of great expansion in your life. This may involve the flowering of a new relationship or project, or a significant development of consciousness that will be of benefit.

Right: A fusty room full of ancient furniture is a hint to spring-clean your attitudes.

A pristine or empty room invites you to furnish it. Here is an opportunity to be creative and transcend your limitations.

Attics and Basements

An attic belongs at the top of a house. As a symbol, it
therefore relates to your head and suggests ideas, aspirations,
and spiritual concerns. Basements, on the other hand, lie
beneath the ground. They represent your unconscious
instincts, the intuitive knowledge that arises from the
depths of your being.

A MIND FULL OF CLUTTER?

Is the attic full of junk? This suggests that you need to be more
discriminating. The dream is
encouraging you to question
opinions you have accepted
unthinkingly. Looking out of an
attic window implies taking an
overview of your situation. Are
you too elevated to see details
clearly? Is your view obstructed?

DOWN IN THE DEPTHS

If you dream about being stuck in
a basement, the message is that
you need to shed light on an issue
about which you are "in the dark."
Exploring a basement can indicate
that you are looking beneath the

surface for deeper understanding. Pay particular attention to any person, animal, or object you discover in a basement. It may symbolize an underlying issue of great importance to your welfare now and in time to come.

Below: **Basements are dark, mysterious places, representing your hidden depths.**

MEETING A FRIGHTENING FIGURE

A recurring dream of meeting a frightening figure in a basement gives you an opportunity to learn something new about yourself. Try going back into the dream scenario and asking this individual if he or she is prepared to talk to you. Very often, you will find that it represents a neglected or angry part of yourself who has been shut away. Invite this figure to become part of your life.

Above: **Peering out of an attic window may imply taking a highly rational view which overlooks basic details.**

Gardens

Gardens in dreams symbolize your natural self. You cannot alter its size, but you can decide how best to cultivate it. Is the garden well-tended, or neglected and full of weeds? Is it neat and formal, or wild and ablaze with color?

FLOWERS

Flowers suggest natural beauty and the joys of the senses. An aspect of your own nature may be flowering, a relationship blossoming. Certain flowers have special significance in dreams. Think of red roses, traditional symbols of passion and romance, or lilies, associated with resurrection.

A single flower that features in a dream may symbolize your fullest potential. It needs to unfold in its own unique way.

Right: **The language of flowers: lilies foretell rebirth, roses declare love.**

TREES

Trees can represent the powerful life force that creates your destiny, just as it transforms an acorn into an oak. What does the particular tree in your dream mean to you? A shelter from the elements, or perhaps the simple pleasures of childhood? A tree bearing fruit can signify the fulfillment of innate potential or the culmination of a creative project.

Above: A scene of pure tranquility. Is it too good to be true? Perfect harmony in a dream can suggest a need to be cautious.

Left: A tree bearing luscious fruit may reflect a period of abundant creativity.

Travel

Dreams about travel carry a message about your emotional and spiritual progress as you journey through life. Your dream trip may involve waiting to move on, taking the wrong road, glimpsing new vistas which draw you on, finally arriving at a destination, or happily exploring an unfamiliar place.

BICYCLING AND WALKING

Dreams about bicycling imply that, using your own energy, you are making a sustained and conscious effort to arrive at your

Above: Losing your way in a dream is the equivalent of doing so in life.

destination. "Cycling" dreams can also emphasize the importance of maintaining a balanced attitude. Are you keeping to the straight and narrow, or veering off course?

GOING IT ALONE

In symbolic language, walking indicates a healthy desire to move at your own pace, feet firmly in touch with the ground. This gives you the opportunity to use your senses and digest the scenery around you. Walking in dreams can also suggest a need to make your own way forward, depending wholly on your own inner resources. Where are you walking to? Is it an uphill journey? Are there obstacles blocking the path?

Below: **A stunning vista like this should encourage optimism about the future.**

Above: **Obstacles blocking your path impede your progress: you are faced with issues in your life which challenge you to become more resourceful.**

Cars

Cars in dreams reveal something about your "drive," or available energy. Are you on the main highway, driving down a side street, looking for somewhere to park, or making erratic progress? Perhaps your car will not start, or refuses to stop. Sometimes cars represent a mechanical way of getting around, implying the need to question your actions.

WHO'S IN CHARGE?

Are you the driver? To dream about being a passenger may mean that you are being driven by somebody else's needs or expectations. The dream is urging you to take control and become a more active participant in your life.

WHAT TYPE OF CAR IS IT?

What does your dream car say about

you? Is it a powerful, exciting sports model, a smooth, stylish sedan, or a more practical, no-nonsense vehicle? Is it old or new? How do you feel about driving this car? Do you need to feel more – or less – like that in your waking life?

Left: **Driving effortlessly through a beautiful landscape – but don't be lulled into a false sense of security. Watch out for obstacles.**

Your dream car? Does it represent unattainable aspirations, or more achievable goals? Are you living in the fast lane or chugging along?

Trains

Dreams about trains indicate that you are traveling along a fixed track, in the same conventional way as everybody else. This suits some people very well. Others, though, may feel frustrated at the lack of freedom to make the choices appropriate to their own individual needs. Notice how you feel about being on this particular train.

IN THE UNDERWORLD

Dreams about traveling on a subway indicate that you are connected to a part of your nature which is hidden deep within your unconscious. Sometimes it implies that in one area of your life, you feel you are being moved along by mysterious forces over which you have little control.

STATIONS

Stations are stopping-off points from where you set out for a new destination. A station in dreams

Left: **Stations epitomize movement and change: in dreams they usually symbolize a transition point on your journey through life.**

Right: **Sometimes you follow a straight track to your destination. This may give you a sense of stability, or it may seem restrictive.**

can therefore symbolize a change of outlook. If you find yourself on the wrong platform for your destination, your dream is a message to warn you that you are heading along the wrong track.

THE ETERNAL TRAIN JOURNEY

Dreaming that you are on a train that fails to stop anywhere may indicate a situation in which you are allowing yourself to be carried along automatically without pausing to consider your options. A train fare that is unrealistically expensive suggests that you are paying too high a price simply in order to go along with the crowd.

Below: **The subway is a metaphor for the secret network of emotions, fears, insights, and beliefs that make you the person you are.**

Flying

Dreams of flying can have several possible meanings. You may be a natural high flier, or find it difficult to get off the ground. Dreams in which you are simply flying along effortlessly, reveling in your freedom from earthly restraints, need no further analysis. All you need do is enjoy this reminder of your spiritual nature.

SPREADING YOUR WINGS

As a positive symbol, flying can mean rising above obstacles or getting a bird's-eye view of a situation. Less auspiciously, it can indicate feeling superior to others,

Left: **From high above the patchwork of your life, you can see how pieces interlock.**

made
easy

Above: **Floating through the air on a warm breeze can offer an experience of freedom from mundane cares and considerations.**

Left: Lofty ideals, inflated opinions, and grand schemes come under the wing of airplane dreams.

or living in a fantasy world and avoiding the realities of everyday life. You must come down to earth.

SOARING TO A HIGHER PLANE

Flying in a plane can signify high ideals that you hold in common with your fellow passengers. Traveling in a huge jet could be a warning against harboring grandiose ideas. If you see the plane crash, it suggests that an idea has run its course, or that you need to bail out. Flying can also imply rapid progress.

Problems with Journeys

Dreams about problematic journeys can have several meanings. Where are you going right now — and how? Are you rushing ahead without first thinking things through? Do you expect too much of yourself?

Below: Dreaming about a sinking ship suggests that powerful forces are undermining your equilibrium.

OUT OF CONTROL

You must leave for the airport but suddenly realize that you have not packed. You forget your passport. You arrive at your chosen destination only to realize that you have left all the windows open at home. Or you arrive at the station only to discover that your train has left. Dreams like these can be triggered by the stress of trying too hard to be in control. A vehicle that crashes often carries a similar meaning.

Above: It can be hard to know which way to turn; one path is the right way for you.

GETTING LOST

You are in unfamiliar territory and cannot find the way home. Or your car is not where you thought you had left it. Dreams of this type suggest that your goals and ambitions are changing but that you have not yet found a new direction. You may benefit from a period of calm reflection.

Right: Where did I leave my car? Life has become a bit of a maze: calm down and center yourself to find the answers you seek.

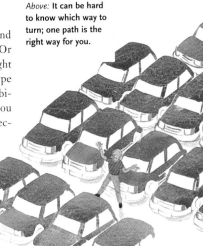

You and Your Body

The physical body is your means of expression in the outer world. Your body in a dream is a symbolic expression of your inner life. Illness is often symptomatic of a conflict between the inner and outer bodies and may therefore be depicted symbolically in dreams long before it manifests physically.

LOSING YOUR TEETH

You realize with horror that your teeth are coming loose or even falling out. Sometimes this dream can be a warning from your "inner" body that you need to pay a visit to your dentist. More commonly, though, it has a symbolic meaning.

GETTING A GRIP

Because teeth are essential for chewing food, they can represent your "bite on life." Losing them can therefore suggest that you feel indecisive or powerless

Above: **Dreams sometimes carry a warning of illness in symbolic form.**

to act. Your dream is encouraging you to be more forceful. Alternatively, you may need to "get your teeth" into something for which you are reluctant to take responsibility.

LETTING YOURSELF DOWN

Losing teeth often reflects a fear that you have failed to project a good self-image and have therefore "lost face." Since being "toothless" is a state normally associated with babies, such dreams can also suggest an immature attitude.

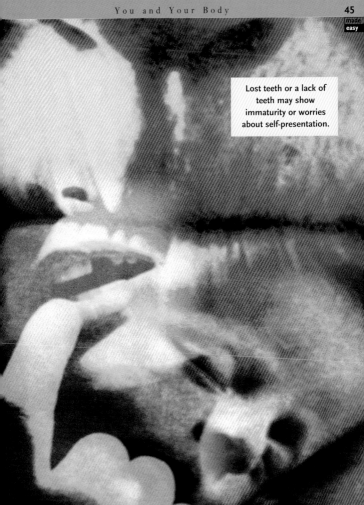

Lost teeth or a lack of teeth may show immaturity or worries about self-presentation.

Clothes and Nudity

Clothing in dreams represents your persona — the appearance you present to others. Wearing clothes chosen for you by someone else suggests that you place too much importance on the image that person has of you. Because you can hide behind your persona, wearing no clothes can often symbolize defenselessness, but can also imply a lack of artifice.

WHAT ARE YOU WEARING?

Are you dressed in sober working attire, or an outrageously sexy outfit? Are your clothes appropriate for the occasion, too formal or not stylish enough? If you are dressed in period costume, what attracts you to that era? Do you currently exhibit those qualities?

THE NAKED TRUTH

You are in a public place and suddenly realize that you are naked. If you take this in your stride, the implication

Below: Inappropriate dress may denote that you do not feel equal to handling a situation.

Right: How you are dressed (or not) relates to issues concerning the image you present to the world at large.

Above: Revealing your assets to the world is not a sign of exhibitionism; rather it suggests you may feel defenceless.

is that you feel comfortable in your skin. Usually, though, the dream suggests that you feel emotionally exposed or vulnerable because you cannot find a suitable role for yourself.

Jewels and Accessories

Jewels in dreams imply something of great value. Gold, being incorruptible, represents that most precious thing of all — your true self. Rings symbolize feelings of wholeness, integrity, or power, but may also signify the "ring of truth."

Left: An overflowing jewel box of sparkling gems may represent an abundance of precious gifts hidden within.

Above: Outsize shoes could be a gentle hint that you have acquired an inflated opinion of yourself.

SHOES

Shoes in dreams often indicate how well you are grounded in reality. Are they sturdy or impractical? Do they fit? Wearing shoes that are too large may imply that you are "too big for your boots." Are you standing in somebody

else's shoes? If the soles need repairing, "soul-work" is called for.

Above: **A lost purse can show panic about personal identity.**

PURSES AND WALLETS

According to Freud, purses symbolize the womb or female genitalia. An alternative explana-tion is that purses usually contain distinctively per-sonal items. Losing your purse can therefore sug-gest feelings of insecurity about your identity. A lost wallet can indicate feelings of being under-valued or a lack of personal power.

Different Parts of the Body

As in waking life, bodily imagery in dreams often serves as a metaphor for certain feelings or attitudes. You can "hold someone at arm's length," feel the pain of "a broken heart," "stand on your own two feet," or have a "gut reaction."

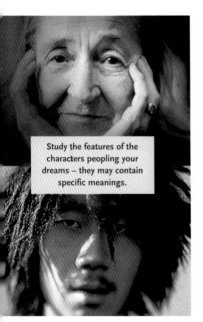

Study the features of the characters peopling your dreams – they may contain specific meanings.

HAIR: Because it grows out of your head, hair can represent ideas. However, hair is also a common symbol for power or sexuality. White hair traditionally signifies wisdom.

NOSE: The nose symbolizes intuition, the ability to "sniff out" the truth. Or is someone being nosy?

HANDS: Hands in dreams can suggest you are getting a grasp on something or that a helping hand is being offered. Sometimes they signify creative ability or "hands-on" involvement.

LEGS: Legs support the body and carry it forward. Weak or injured legs in a dream can imply that you haven't a leg to stand on, or can go no farther in a situation. Try to ground yourself.

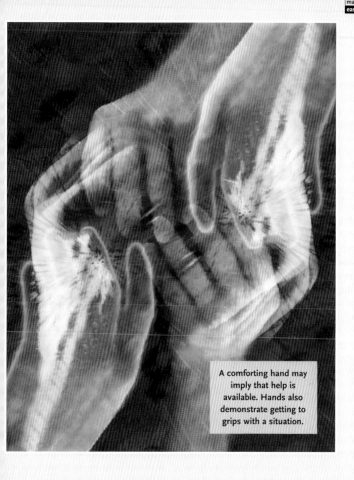

A comforting hand may imply that help is available. Hands also demonstrate getting to grips with a situation.

Sexuality

Freud believed that sexual dreams were symptomatic of repressed primitive urges. Carl Jung subsequently found that such dreams say something about the relationship between the masculine and feminine aspects of the psyche. From this point of view, sexual dreams are a metaphor for creativity.

THE INNER PARTNER

You dream of making love with somebody of the opposite sex, an actual lover, a friend, a relative, or a colleague. This could simply indicate sexual frustration. Otherwise, ask yourself what you admire, or even dislike about that person. The dream is an invitation to connect with an unknown side of your nature which the dream partner happens to represent.

SAME-SEX RELATIONSHIPS

Dreaming about sex with a person of the same gender does not indicate homosexuality. It means that

Left: A sexual dream does not always reflect desire: it may be a connection to your lover's personal qualities.

Right: **A sexual dream may reflect a yearning for excitement, or a need to be more creative.**

you are trying to get in touch with your own feminine or masculine energy. We have little idea of what it means, psychologically, to be truly masculine or feminine. Many people are searching for the answers in their dreams.

Feminine energy is symbolically associated with qualities like acceptance, compassion, and relatedness. Masculine energy is more thrusting, goal-orientated, and analytic. Dreams reveal how these two forces interact within us.

Left: **Erotic dreams featuring a partner of the same sex imply a need to embrace your masculine or feminine nature.**

Animals

Good relationship with your "animal instincts" is the basis of psychic health. Dreams about animals therefore carry a message about how strongly you are linked with the natural world. According to the Native American tradition, a dream animal has special wisdom to offer the dreamer.

Right: Dreams of animals often carry a message about your relationship with the natural world and therefore indicate whether you are on good terms with your instincts.

DOMESTICATED ANIMALS

Cats and dogs, the most common domesticated animals, share our houses, our routines, and sometimes our meals. In dreams they therefore represent our natural socializing instincts. Are the pets in your dream well cared-for, neglected, or aggressive?

CATS

Cats can see in the dark and in dreams are therefore associated with feminine, intuitive energy.

Because they are given to unearthly caterwauling when in heat, they can also represent both sensuality and other-worldliness. Cats expect their needs to be met and may therefore indicate a need for healthy selfishness or greater independence. Might you be catty?

Above: **Cats stand for the selfish, sensual, mysterious, or intuitive.**

DOGS

The dog, "man's best friend," traditionally represents masculine energy. In dreams dogs can symbolize loyalty and "doglike" devotion, as well as "dogged perseverance" or unbridled energy. Black dogs may imply depression. Is your dream dog a ferocious rottweiler or a docile lap dog? Do you recognize those qualities in yourself? Do you lead a dog's life?

Right: **A rottweiler may represent great strength or vicious tendencies.**

Jungle Creatures

Every day you fulfill your responsibilities as a family member, a worker, a citizen. What, then, happens to the untrammeled, undomesticated aspects of yourself? If you do not express these instincts in some appropriate form, they may prowl around your dreams in the guise of wild animals.

LIONS

As "king of the jungle," the lion is associated with the masculine aspect of life and with

Above: **The lion is a subtext for dignified, contained power that could be unleashed to devastating effect.**

qualities such as generosity, courage, and regal pride. A caged and unhappy lion in a dream implies that you are

Above: **Caged beasts can reflect
a reluctance to liberate the forceful
side of your nature.**

afraid of your own power and
therefore keep it firmly locked
away in case it should wreak havoc.

TIGERS

Tigers represent a vibrant aspect
of feminine energy: "Nature red in
tooth and claw." Because they are
solitary creatures of awesome
power, dreaming about a tiger can
imply that you need to find the
strength to go your own way. You
may have to be fierce, or even
ruthless, in order to achieve a sat-
isfactory outcome.

Right: **Tigers can represent a
commitment to fighting
for what you believe in.**

Snakes

In the Judeo-Christian tradition, snakes have always been associated with sexuality and evil. While a snake may be a phallic symbol in dreams, it also has other, very different meanings. You need to find the one which most accurately reflects your circumstances.

INTUITIVE WISDOM

The serpent in the Garden of Eden brought knowledge of good and evil to Eve. Snakes can therefore symbolize intuitive, feminine wisdom. In Eastern philosophy, snakes symbolize the life-force, or *kundalini*, coiled at the base of the

手厥陰心包經之圖

Far left: Snakes ca mean temptation. Adam and Eve we led astray by the Devil in the guise of a snake.

Left: In the East, life force is believe to flow in channel along the spine. Snakes symbolize this force.

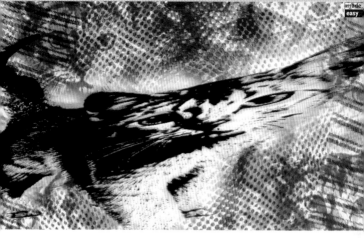

Because they are given to unearthly caterwauling when in heat, they can also represent both sensuality and other-worldliness. Cats expect their needs to be met and may therefore indicate a need for healthy selfishness or greater independence. Might you be catty?

Above: **Cats stand for the selfish, sensual, mysterious, or intuitive.**

DOGS

The dog, "man's best friend," traditionally represents masculine energy. In dreams dogs can symbolize loyalty and "doglike" devotion, as well as "dogged perseverance" or unbridled energy. Black dogs may imply depression. Is your dream dog a ferocious rottweiler or a docile lap dog? Do you recognize those qualities in yourself? Do you lead a dog's life?

Right: **A rottweiler may represent great strength or vicious tendencies.**

Jungle Creatures

Every day you fulfill your responsibilities as a family member, a worker, a citizen. What, then, happens to the untrammeled, undomesticated aspects of yourself? If you do not express these instincts in some appropriate form, they may prowl around your dreams in the guise of wild animals.

LIONS

As "king of the jungle," the lion is associated with the masculine aspect of life and with

Above: **The lion is a subtext for dignified, contained power that could be unleashed to devastating effect.**

qualities such as generosity, courage, and regal pride. A caged and unhappy lion in a dream implies that you are

Above: **Caged beasts can reflect
a reluctance to liberate the forceful
side of your nature.**

afraid of your own power and
therefore keep it firmly locked
away in case it should wreak havoc.

TIGERS

Tigers represent a vibrant aspect
of feminine energy: "Nature red in
tooth and claw." Because they are
solitary creatures of awesome
power, dreaming about a tiger can
imply that you need to find the
strength to go your own way. You
may have to be fierce, or even
ruthless, in order to achieve a sat-
isfactory outcome.

Right: **Tigers can represent a
commitment to fighting
for what you believe in.**

Snakes

In the Judeo-Christian tradition, snakes have always been associated with sexuality and evil. While a snake may be a phallic symbol in dreams, it also has other, very different meanings. You need to find the one which most accurately reflects your circumstances.

INTUITIVE WISDOM

The serpent in the Garden of Eden brought knowledge of good and evil to Eve. Snakes can therefore symbolize intuitive, feminine wisdom. In Eastern philosophy, snakes symbolize the life-force, or *kundalini*, coiled at the base of the

Far left: **Snakes ca mean temptation. Adam and Eve we led astray by the Devil in the guise of a snake.**

Left: **In the East, life force is believe to flow in channel along the spine. Snakes symbolize this force.**

Above: **Cramming in a victim. Snakes can depict potential for destruction.**

spine. Awakening this pure, psychic energy leads to spiritual enlightenment and improved mental and physical health.

HEALING OR POISONOUS?

Because it sloughs its skin, the snake is associated with rejuvenation and was the emblem of the Greek god of healing. A dream snake may therefore signify a process of transformation in your life. Many snakes, though, are poisonous. Do you harbor venomous attitudes, or have you come across them in others?

Left: **Your dream snake may be a sign that you are undergoing a transformation.**

Fish, Frogs, and Insects

Our dreams often feature creatures that swim, fly, hop, or crawl around and disturb us. They represent primitive forces hidden deep within the psyche, where they exert a profound influence on our attitudes.

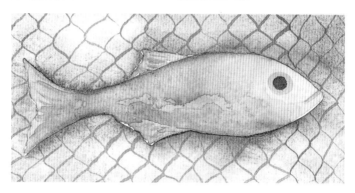

FISH

Catching fish in dreams indicates "fishing up" new insights or ideas from the depths of the unconscious. Alternatively, you can be a "fish out of water" or involved with someone who is "a cold fish". Is something "fishy" going on? Fish

Above: If a fish swims through your dream, there are many interpretations.

as phallic symbols imply fertility. Sharks in dreams usually symbolize dangerous, predatory forces in the depths of the psyche. Fishes also signify spirituality – early Christians used the fish as a symbol of Christianity – and may represent your "inmost divinity" or wholeness.

FROGS

When the princess kissed the frog, he became a handsome prince. Dreams of frogs can therefore imply finding hidden beauty or meaning in unexpected places. Frogs are also associated with the reproductive powers of nature and, accordingly, with burgeoning new life.

Above: **Being so fertile, frogs can imply a wish to procreate.**

INSECTS

Insects in dreams often signify that something is "bugging" you. A spider industriously weaving its web can suggest creativity, or the workings of destiny. Less positively, it implies an over-possessive attitude. Wasps can signify being stung by "waspish" attitudes.

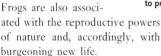

Below: **Spiders weave intricate webs, and their appearance can signify manipulative behavior.**

Nature

According to St Bernard, "One learns more in the woods than in books; the trees and the rocks will teach you things that you would not otherwise be able to understand". In our dreams, too, nature provides the symbols through which we can gain wisdom and self-understanding.

WATER

Life begins in water. In dreams water may therefore represent the fertile realm of the unconscious from whose depths emerges new growth, healing or an outpouring of creativity. Water also symbolizes emotional energy. It can circulate freely, build up slowly to form a reservoir, gradually wear away obstacles, or freeze over.

WATER POWER

Dreams about being immersed in water suggest that you are in touch with your feelings or

Right: **Being enveloped by calm, lapping waters shows you have achieved emotional balance and stability.**

Seas boiling up into a tidal wave sound an alarm about the danger of being overcome by emotions.

happily 'in the swim'. If a tidal wave threatens, the dream may be warning you against being engulfed by your emotions.

RIVERS OF TIME

Rivers symbolize the flow of your life during the passage of time. Because rivers often mark boundaries, dreams about crossing a river imply that you are at a transition point, moving from one state to another. Are you going with the flow or battling against it?

Above: A meandering dream river may be calling for a relaxed, unhurried approach.

Fire

Fire is commonly linked with passion and libido. You may have a fiery temperament or be "fired up" with enthusiasm for a person or a cause. Fire also implies purification, the burning away of the dross in order to make way for something better. In dreams it can therefore symbolize transformation.

TOO HOT TO HANDLE
Some dreams carry a warning about the destructive aspect of fiery energy. You can be consumed with rage or become the victim of your own uncontrolled passions. An explosion implies an outburst of repressed feelings which have finally "overheated."

HEALTH MATTERS
Certain bodily symptoms such as a high temperature or raised blood pressure can be reflected in dreams about fire. If you dream that your house is on

Left: Smoldering passions or an all-consuming enthusiasm can spark off fiery dreams.

fire, you may therefore benefit from a health check. Or perhaps you are "burned out" and needing rest and recuperation.

NO SMOKE WITHOUT FIRE
Dreams of a smoking fire may indicate that you are smoldering with suppressed anger or resentment and in danger of exploding.

Right: **Dreaming about a burning house may indicate physical "heat" symptoms such as high blood pressure.**

Below: **Red-hot lava, spurting out of an erupting volcano, is allied to an uncontrolled emotional outburst.**

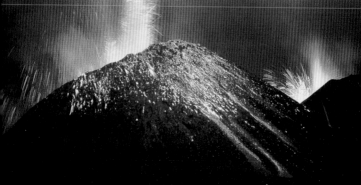

Mountains

Because mountains represent the meeting place between heaven and earth, they have traditionally been associated with spiritual aspiration. Reaching the summit or peak therefore symbolizes enlightenment. Most dreams of mountains, though, have less rarefied meanings.

UNREALISTIC AIMS

If you are trying to achieve a goal that feels like "uphill work," you will probably dream about climbing a steep mountain. Meeting obstacles that prevent you from

A mountain summit shrouded in mist may show a hidden yearning for peak experience.

making further progress suggests that you need more determination – or possibly a different way of accomplishing your objective. Are you attempting to climb too high?

AT THE PINNACLE

Dreaming that you have arrived at the top of a mountain may sig-nify reaching the peak of achievement. Such dreams can also indicate that you have reached a point where you need to stop and take an overview of your life. How does your situation look from this perspective?

Right: **A secure foothold could signify finding the next step in a tricky situation.**

Below: **Panoramic views indicate that you are able to see the big picture.**

Common Anxiety Dreams

Dreams in which you feel anxious are a message about the
need to deal with fears which are holding you back. Often,
they illustrate a conflict between an ideal you cherish and the
reality you are reluctant to face. Anxiety dreams can also
indicate "unfinished emotional business" arising from past
traumatic experiences.

TAKING AN EXAM
In most "exam" dreams, you suddenly realize, in a panic, that you
have done no work and will be
unable to answer the questions.
Perhaps you haven't even studied
the subject at all. Oddly enough, if
you are actually about to take an
exam, your dream may be an
omen of success!

AM I GOOD ENOUGH?
This type of dream usually
implies a concern about your ability to "make the grade." Are you
unduly worried about being seen
as inadequate? Are you involved
in any situation in which you feel
you are being tested?

Above: **The awful sinking feeling,
of arriving at an exam unprepared,
reveals fears of inadequacy.**

Right: **Tripling in the final lap costs you the race... it could imply that you are secretly frightened of being a success.**

BE KIND TO YOURSELF!

If you tend to be a perfectionist, your "exam" dream is a message that you harbour unrealistic expectations of yourself. It is encouraging you to be less critical. Relax! Accept that you can only do your best. Life is not a test!

Falling From a Height

You are somewhere high up, unable to move, terrified of
falling. This common dream has several different meanings.
Are you afraid of falling in love, falling on hard times, or
falling into temptation? If you feel you must always be in
control of events, the dream is urging you to learn to trust.

PRIDE COMES BEFORE A FALL

"Falling" dreams can indicate that you are overconfident about your abilities, or even a little arrogant. They carry a warning that unless you adopt a more realistic attitude, you may be heading for a fall. Such dreams can also reflect concern about loss of status.

LIVING IN YOUR HEAD

Are you ruled by your head at the expense of your heart? Do you tend to live in a world of your own? If so, your dream is alerting you to the dangers of losing touch

Left: Plunging into a black abyss, securely tied to a rope, suggests that you can safely step out into the unknown.

with the ground beneath your feet. One common dream is that of being in a very high place, hanging on by your fingertips. This suggests that you are afraid of losing your grip. The implication is that you need to relax your efforts to maintain the status quo and to develop a more easy-going attitude.

Below: **Dreams of falling may symbolize your need to come down to earth.**

Being Pursued

Whatever you are running away from in a dream is something you actually need to turn and face. Your pursuer usually represents a part of yourself you are unwilling to acknowledge, often because you are afraid of it. If an animal is chasing you, imagine how it would feel to be that creature.

THE ENEMY WITHIN

If your pursuer is someone you know in waking life, how do you feel about them? What are their most striking qualities? The dream is urging you to recognize that these qualities are also yours. If you can integrate them, you will enrich your personality immeasurably.

THREATS FROM OUTSIDE

Unknown pursuers symbolize forces that are difficult to come to terms with. Dreams of a frantic flight from a shadowy,

Above: You may fight shy of admitting certain things about yourself, which then keep coming after you.

Above: **A pursuer may embody qualities that it would benefit you to develop.**

Right: **Facing your pursuer marks a determination to stand up to problems.**

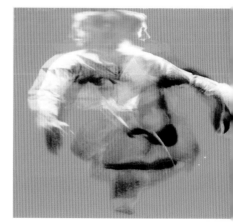

vaguely threatening figure are often connected with a situation or person that you are trying to avoid. Stop hiding and start to tackle the issue head-on – and the worrying dream will not recur.

Colors

Colors represent the diversity of your personality: the more of them you incorporate, the more colorful your life will be. Are the colors in your dreams bright or muted? Notice how you feel about them. Here are some qualities traditionally associated with colors.

BLACK AND WHITE

Black symbolizes the unconscious, or unknown quantities. Sometimes it indicates depression. White stands for that which is positive, pure, or transcendent.

RED

Red is the color of sexuality, passion and anger. It signifies self-confidence and vitality.

YELLOW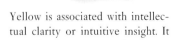

Yellow is associated with intellectual clarity or intuitive insight. It may also denote cowardice.

Above: **Dreams awash with vibrant colors, like Gaugin's paintings of Tahiti, suggest intensity of experience.**

Right: **The shiny metallics of gold and silver represent the opposing, yet complementary, forces in life – sun and moon, male and female.**

GREEN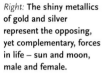

Green, the color of nature, represents youthfulness, energy, and renewed life force – but can also imply envy.

BLUE

Blue, the color of heaven, usually represents spirituality. It can also suggest sadness, as in 'feeling blue'.

SILVER

Silver, the color of the moon, represents the cyclical, feminine principle of life.

PURPLE

Purple is the regal color, associated with power and pride. It can symbolize stateliness, wisdom, experience, and formality.

GOLD

Gold, associated with the sun and the masculine principle, also signifies the highest possible value. It hints at spiritual richness.

Numbers

Numbers are considered by many to be the fundamental principle of the universe. Spiritual systems, esoteric traditions, and modern science all use the symbolism of numbers to try and penetrate the mystery of creation. The numbers one to four frequently occur in dreams.

ONE

One is the number of the underlying principle from which diversity emerges. It represents oneness with life, harmony, order, or a new beginning. It is the base unit and can therefore represent your inmost self.

TWO

Two symbolizes duality, two opposing aspects of a situation. It can imply balance or necessary conflict. Two of anything in a dream accentuates its importance in your life.

THREE

Three, as the number of the Trinity, can symbolize creative power. Carl Jung felt that, because the Trinity lacks the feminine element, three represents something that is not yet complete. It may also indicate a resolution of a particular conflict between two opposing forces.

FOUR

Consider the four seasons, four elements, four quarters to a whole. Four means stability, wholeness, and completion.

A specific number of similar dream symbols has a special meaning.

Birth and Death

Dreams about birth and death indicate profound change.
Throughout life, your energy undergoes a process of
transformation. Outworn attitudes must die so that new
aspects of yourself can be born. These dreams imply the
need to accept the ongoing, natural process of change
which is fundamental to life.

BIRTH

Birth in dreams can signify a new stage of your life's journey, the birth of a new perspective or a fresh insight. Being pregnant for an unnaturally long time suggests a reluctance to allow the next phase to begin.

Birth can be a metaphor
for the conception
of ideas, or a revision
of attitudes.

Left: **Dreams of pregnancy may reflect
the desire for a child, or herald new
developments in your life.**

DEATH

Dreams of death are not to be
taken literally. They are a symbolic – and positive – message
that you have reached the culmination of a cycle. What does the
dead person in the dream represent to you? This is the part of
you that needs to "die." Let it go
– and become more of the person
you were always meant to be.

Above: **The final stage in life.
Dreaming about it means that a cycle in
your life has reached a natural conclusion.**

Index